Original title:
The Whispering Pines

Copyright © 2024 Swan Charm
All rights reserved.

Author: Kätriin Kaldaru
ISBN HARDBACK: 978-9916-79-714-3
ISBN PAPERBACK: 978-9916-79-715-0
ISBN EBOOK: 978-9916-79-716-7

Hush of the Woodland Spirits

In the glade where shadows play,
Whispers of the leaves do sway.
Silent echoes, soft and clear,
Nature's beauty, drawing near.

Moonlit paths of silver light,
Guide the heart through gentle night.
Mossy beds, a tranquil rest,
In the calm, we feel our best.

Beneath the branches, secrets weave,
Stories that the stars believe.
Each soft sigh, each rustle near,
A timeless dance, a sacred sphere.

Living shadows twist and twine,
Nature's spirits, pure and fine.
In the silence, we discover,
The magic hidden, like no other.

In this realm, where calm prevails,
Whispers ride the gentle gales.
Hush now, let the world fade away,
In the woodland, we wish to stay.

Soliloquy Beneath the Green Ceiling

Leaves like parchment overhead,
In the woods, where thoughts are fed.
A gentle breeze begins to speak,
Words of wisdom, soft and meek.

Between the trunks, a hush unfolds,
Tales of life that nature holds.
In this sanctuary of peace,
The soul finds voice, the heart's release.

Sunlight dapples through the boughs,
Painting dreams upon our brows.
Each stroke of warmth, a gentle guide,
In tranquility, we can abide.

Whispers of the earth awake,
Bearing gifts of joy they make.
Time stands still beneath this dome,
Here in nature, we are home.

With each breath, we start to blend,
Life and nature, hand in hand.
Underneath this leafy eaves,
We find solace in the leaves.

Sighs of the Timbered Giants

Stand tall, oh giants of the wood,
In their shade, we find our good.
Whispered tales of ages past,
Echoes in the air, so vast.

Branches sway in soft embrace,
Guardians of this sacred space.
Ancient voices, wise and deep,
Secrets in the silence keep.

Roots that burrow, strong and wide,
Holding stories, deep inside.
Each ring a passage of the years,
Composing history with our tears.

Through the mist and morning dew,
Life unfolds in every hue.
Timber giants watch the night,
Guardians of the fading light.

As shadows stretch and stars ignite,
They whisper softly, pure delight.
In their presence, we can feel,
The heartbeat of the earth, so real.

Conversations with the Twilight Sky

As day retreats, the sky ignites,
Colors merge in wondrous sights.
A canvas filled with dreams and sighs,
In the hush where twilight lies.

Clouds drift freely, thoughts unwind,
In the silence, grace we find.
Stars emerge, a twinkling dance,
Inviting all to take a chance.

Softly spoken, winds will carry,
Gentle breezes, light and airy.
Every star a distant tale,
A cosmic song, the nightingale.

Twilight's glow, a fleeting friend,
In her arms, we blend and mend.
With each breath, the world's a dream,
In the stillness, thoughts will stream.

As the day turns into night,
We find peace in fading light.
Conversations with the sky,
Whispered joys that never die.

Quietude Beneath the Sky

In the stillness, shadows play,
Underneath the sun's soft ray.
Clouds drift lazily, minds unwind,
Peaceful moments, rare to find.

A breeze carries whispers clear,
Nature's secrets, close and near.
Birds sing sweetly, hearts take flight,
In quietude, all feels right.

The sun dips low, painting hues,
Golden glimmers, evening's muse.
Stars awaken, a gentle sigh,
In twilight's calm, beneath the sky.

Softly falls the nighttime chill,
In the quiet, souls are still.
Dreams take form in shadows deep,
In peacefulness, we drift to sleep.

Awake to dawn, light anew,
In quietude, embrace what's true.
Life unfolds in careful grace,
Beneath the sky, a sacred space.

Guardians of the Ancient Grove

In the heart of woods so old,
Trees stand tall, their stories told.
Roots entwined, a silent bond,
Guardians watch, ever fond.

Soft moss carpets the forest floor,
Whispers echo, nature's lore.
Creatures wander, shadows flit,
In this grove, all things fit.

Sunlight dapples through the leaves,
Filling hearts with gentle ease.
Life abounds in vibrant hues,
In this realm, the ancient muse.

Time stands still, a sacred place,
Where the spirit finds its pace.
Echoes of the past remain,
Guardians soothe with soft refrain.

As twilight falls, the stars ignite,
In the grove, a soft delight.
Whispers linger in the air,
Guardians watch, forever care.

Timeless Watchers of the Dawn

In the hush before the day,
Mountains rise, holding sway.
With the first light, shadows flee,
Timeless watchers, wild and free.

Birds awaken, songs arise,
Painting echoes in the skies.
Crisp air beckons, life anew,
In dawn's embrace, dreams come true.

Morning dew like diamonds shine,
Nature's beauty, pure, divine.
Each heartbeat in sync with day,
Timeless watchers guide our way.

Golden rays touch every seed,
Filling hearts with hope and need.
Life's journey begins again,
In the dawn, where love has been.

As the sun ascends the height,
World awakens, bursting bright.
Timeless watchers nod with grace,
In dawn's glow, we find our place.

Whispers in the Rustling Leaves

In the forest, a soft breeze,
Carries tales through rustling leaves.
Nature speaks in gentle sighs,
Whispers shared beneath the skies.

Branches dance in playful sway,
Each crackle tells of yesterday.
Time unfurls in every turn,
In quiet songs, our spirits yearn.

Sunlight filters through the green,
Creating patterns, pure and serene.
Life unfolds in softest hues,
In whispers, nature's secret muse.

Evenings come with starlit grace,
A quiet calm, a sacred space.
Every rustle holds a tale,
In the leaves, where dreams set sail.

As night descends with velvet veil,
Nature breathes, a soothing tale.
Whispers linger in the night,
In rustling leaves, our hearts take flight.

Where Silence Embraces the Sky

In the hush of twilight's grace,
Stars awaken, dreams embrace.
Whispers of the night unfold,
Silent stories to be told.

Clouds drift in a gentle swirl,
Moonlight dances, shadows twirl.
Nature breathes in soft repose,
In this stillness, peace bestows.

Echoes linger, nightbirds sing,
Lost in thoughts that twilight brings.
A canvas stretched, serene and wide,
Where silence meets the sky's tide.

Veils of stars, a shimmering sheet,
Beneath the heavens, hearts retreat.
In this quiet, souls align,
Where silence reigns, pure and divine.

Memories Held in a Bristlecone

Ancient roots in weathered stone,
Bristlecones whisper, time alone.
In their rings, the ages show,
Tales of winds that come and go.

Underneath the endless blue,
Their sturdy branches hold the view.
Peaceful guardians of the past,
In their embrace, moments last.

Seasons change, yet they stand tall,
Witness to the rise and fall.
Memories wrapped in bark and shade,
In their presence, time won't fade.

Each needle pointing to the sky,
In solitude, they wonder why.
Nature's secrets in their core,
Bristlecones share forevermore.

The Language of Starlit Pines

Whispers stir in moonlit air,
Pines converse without a care.
In the dark, their voices blend,
Nature's songs that never end.

Needles rustle, shadows sway,
Speaking tales of night and day.
Stars above join in the tune,
A symphony beneath the moon.

Branches arch in soft embrace,
Carrying the night's grace.
In their hearts, the stories grow,
The language only they can know.

Wind whispers secrets, soft and shy,
Pines reply with a gentle sigh.
Together in this sacred rite,
The language of the starlit night.

Crescendo of Nature's Choir

As dawn breaks, the chorus wakes,
Birds take flight, the earth quakes.
With each note, the world revives,
Nature's breath, it sings and thrives.

Streams babble in joyful spree,
Leaves join in, a symphony.
Whispers from the rustling green,
In this concert, peace is seen.

Mountains echo, valleys hum,
The earth responds; a vibrant drum.
In harmony, the wild unfolds,
Tales of life in rhythms bold.

Crickets strum as night descends,
In twilight's hush, the music bends.
Every creature lends a voice,
In nature's choir, hearts rejoice.

Shadows and Stories in the Trees

In the twilight, whispers blend,
Ancient tales the branches lend.
Leaves rustle soft, secrets unfold,
In shadows deep, the stories told.

Moonlight dances through the boughs,
Calmly tracing sacred vows.
Each knot and twist a memory,
In the heart of where we'll be.

Roots entwined beneath the ground,
Echoes of the lost, profound.
Nature's voice, a timeless song,
In this place, we all belong.

Glimmers speak of what has passed,
Windswept dreams that hold us fast.
Every sapling's gentle sway,
Calls the night and beckons day.

So listen close, let silence weave,
In the trees, we dare believe.
Shadows play their endless part,
In the whisper of the heart.

Murmuring Among the Moss

Deep in the woods where shadows creep,
Secrets hide and silence keeps.
Moss blankets stones, a verdant hue,
Whispers cradle the morning dew.

Gentle breezes, soft and low,
Call to me, they ebb and flow.
Murmurs of life, so rich and rare,
In quiet corners, beyond compare.

Ferns unfurl like emerald dreams,
In emerald worlds where sunlight beams.
Every footstep, careful, light,
Stirs the calm of nature's night.

Hidden paths through tangled vines,
Echoes of the earth's designs.
Listen deep, let stillness reign,
Feel the pulse of every vein.

Mossy carpets, old and wise,
Hold the memory of the skies.
In these whispers, I find peace,
Amidst the green, my spirit's lease.

The Night's Quiet Reverie

Underneath a blanket of stars,
Silence wraps the world in bars.
Dreams take flight on moonlit beams,
As the night unfolds its themes.

Gentle sighs from shadows near,
Secrets linger, crystal clear.
In the hush, the heart can find,
All the thoughts left far behind.

Crickets sing their soft refrain,
Notes that dance like gentle rain.
Each moment held in twilight's glow,
As the quiet starts to flow.

Stars above in velvet skies,
Whispers shimmer in our eyes.
Time slows down, we breathe it in,
In the calm, new worlds begin.

Night's embrace, a tranquil space,
In the darkness, we discover grace.
Every heartbeat sings a tune,
In the reverie of the moon.

Whispers from the Woodland

In the forest's tender hold,
Nature speaks in secrets told.
With every rustle, every sigh,
Whispers float like spirits nigh.

Saplings stretch towards the light,
Murmurs linger, pure and bright.
Leaves like pages turn and swell,
In the wind, a wondrous spell.

Crimson berries softly gleam,
Nature's bounty flows like dream.
Every path a story keeps,
In the woods where silence sleeps.

Footfalls light on forest floor,
Echoing dreams forevermore.
With every breath, we find anew,
In woodland whispers, life rings true.

So seek the shade, let shadows play,
In nature's heart, we'll find our way.
Among the trees, in every glance,
Whispers weave a sacred dance.

Embrace of the Evergreen Canopy

Tall pines whisper secrets soft,
Underneath their verdant cloak.
The sunlight filters down aloft,
As nature's beauty gently spoke.

In shadows cool, the ferns unfold,
Green tendrils dance with the breeze.
Stories of the earth retold,
In rustling leaves, there's sweet release.

Mossy carpets cradle shy,
Woodland creatures find their way.
Beneath the vast, embracing sky,
A tranquil heart is here to stay.

Birdsong echoes through the trees,
A melody of peace and grace.
In the embrace of the tall leaves,
Time slows down in this sacred space.

Here in the grove, the world feels right,
Nature's hymn, a soothing balm.
Wrapped within this emerald light,
Serenity whispers a calming psalm.

Gentle Messages from the Timber

In twilight's glow, the woods do sigh,
Each branch a letter, sent in time.
Carved in bark, the tales fly by,
In whispers soft, the echoes rhyme.

Leaves murmur secrets to the breeze,
Carried far on wings of flight.
Underneath the ancient trees,
Every heartbeat feels so light.

Tales of seasons etched in grain,
Growth that mirrors life's own dance.
In every storm, in every rain,
The timber sways, a graceful chance.

Light spills through gaps, a gentle glow,
Kissing roots that hold the ground.
In nature's heart, we come to know,
That peace is in the silence found.

Each rustling leaf, a voice so clear,
In nature's choir, we find our role.
Messages from timber here,
Teach the way to a fuller soul.

Sonnet of the Starlit Glade

Beneath the stars, the glade awakes,
Moonlight dances on the dew.
In this realm, the heart partakes,
Of peace so pure, and joys anew.

The nightingale sings soft and low,
Under a blanket of twinkling lights.
In shadows deep, dreams start to flow,
As magic threads through tranquil nights.

Whispers of love drift on the breeze,
As the world hushes in the glow.
A serenade through ancient trees,
Where mysteries of the cosmos flow.

Embrace the silence, let it seep,
Into the core, where wild dreams dwell.
In starlit glades, the heart can leap,
Finding solace in nature's spell.

So linger here, where night unfolds,
And let the glade wrap you in peace.
In starlit skies, the heart beholds,
Endless wonders that never cease.

Hidden Harmonies in the Grove

In the grove, where shadows play,
Soft whispers weave through ancient roots.
The songs of life in bright array,
Echo sweetly, among the shoots.

Colorful blooms, a canvas wide,
In delicate folds, the petals lay.
Nature's brushstrokes coincide,
Creating harmony, come what may.

Hidden paths, where spirits roam,
In careful steps, the heart aligns.
Among the branches, find your home,
In rhythms found where sunlight shines.

A chorus sung by wind and tree,
The gentle rustle, a soothing sound.
In every note, there's unity,
In the grove, true peace is found.

So wander deep, let worries fade,
In hidden harmonies, life thrives.
In the stillness, joyful cascade,
The essence of nature always survives.

Beneath the Elder's Gaze

Beneath the elder's gaze, we stand,
In whispers soft, the stories grand.
Each wrinkle holds a tale untold,
Of moments lost and memories bold.

The branches sway, a silent choir,
Their shadows dance, a fleeting fire.
Together we roam, the past in our heart,
Guided by wisdom, never apart.

In twilight's glow, the night descends,
As stars emerge, like ancient friends.
The elder watches, a guardian still,
With gentle strength, our fears to quell.

Underneath this sky so vast,
We honor those who've long since passed.
With each soft leaf that stirs in flight,
We weave their tales into the night.

Beneath the elder's gaze, we learn,
The fires of love will always burn.
In every heartbeat, we find our place,
Within the shelter of its embrace.

Forgotten Trails and Timeless Tales

In forgotten trails where shadows creep,
The echoes of time in silence seep.
Whispers of wind, through branches glide,
Where ancient paths in memory bide.

Timeless tales of love and strife,
Carved in the earth, the stories of life.
With every step, the past reclaims,
The laughter, the tears, the tender names.

Under the boughs, the secrets sigh,
A tapestry woven with each goodbye.
The earth bears witness to dreams once spun,
In the heart of the forest, all are one.

Each stone a marker of moments lost,
In the quiet woods, we count the cost.
Yet hope still dances in the soft light,
Guiding our souls through the sweet night.

As dawn breaks forth with gentle grace,
We walk the trails, still we embrace.
In every shadow, in every tale,
Lives the spirit of the forgotten trail.

Lament of the Lost Path

In the lament of the lost path, we sigh,
Searching for echoes of days gone by.
Where footsteps once danced on this worn ground,
A silence now reigns, a sorrow profound.

Each turn of the trail, a memory fades,
In shadows and light, the heart wades.
The flowers once bloomed in colors so bright,
Now whisper their woes in the fading light.

Beneath the arching trees, whispers call,
Yet in the stillness, I fear I'll fall.
For every lost path hides stories untold,
Of journeys completed, and dreams left cold.

With heavy heart, I tread the way,
Each step a reminder of yesterday.
In the rustle of leaves, I hear the plea,
To remember the path that once set me free.

Yet in this lament, a spark still glows,
For every end always sows a rose.
In the depths of despair, hope shall arise,
Guiding the lost beneath starlit skies.

The Gentle Caress of Wind

The gentle caress of wind on skin,
Whispers of nature, where dreams begin.
Through fields and valleys, breezes flow,
A symphony sweet, a tranquil show.

With every gust, the trees will sway,
In harmony, they dance and play.
The secrets carried in each soft breeze,
Speak of moments and memories that tease.

When twilight looms and shadows creep,
The wind embraces, and the world sleeps.
With every breath, a story unfolds,
A journey of hearts, both young and old.

In whispers, the wind sings of love,
A melody sweet as the stars above.
With every rustle, a promise made,
To guide our spirits, never to fade.

The gentle caress of wind shall remain,
In every heart, through joy and pain.
For in its embrace, we find our way,
As love transcends, come what may.

Nature's Breath in the Tall Trees

Whispers in the leaves do sway,
Carried softly, night and day.
Sunlight dances on the ground,
Nature's breath in every sound.

Branches stretch to greet the sky,
In their shade, the moments fly.
Gentle rustle, soft and sweet,
Life awakens at their feet.

Roots entwined in soil's embrace,
Hold the stories of this place.
Boughs that cradle birds in song,
Where the heartbeat feels so strong.

In the breeze, a fleeting tune,
Echoes with the rising moon.
Every shadow tells a tale,
Of the storm, the sun, the hail.

Nature's ink paints every scene,
In hues of green, pure and serene.
Time stands still in this domain,
Where the heart finds peace again.

The Enigma of Wooden Giants

Mighty towers touch the sky,
Guardians where the eagles fly.
Ancient trunks with wisdom hold,
Stories whispered, secrets told.

Knots and rings, a life untold,
In their presence, we behold.
Veins of bark, a map of years,
Echoing the laughter, tears.

In twilight's glow, they stand proud,
Silhouettes against the cloud.
Serenading with the wind,
Nature's pact will never end.

As shadows stretch and daylight dims,
A tapestry of nature's hymns.
Footsteps soft on forest floor,
Amongst the giants, we explore.

Echoes drift like dreams on air,
In the stillness, peace lays bare.
Beneath their gaze, the world feels right,
In their embrace, hearts ignite.

Luminescence of Dusk and Dawn

In the hush of morning's glow,
Colors blend, a gentle show.
Softly waking, nature sighs,
As the sun begins to rise.

Golden light on dew-kissed blades,
Shimmers through the forest glades.
Fleeting moments, calm and bright,
Haunting whispers of the night.

As the day begins to fade,
Violet hues of dusk invade.
Stars emerge from twilight's thread,
In the silence, dreams are spread.

Crickets chirp a soothing song,
Nature's chords where we belong.
Daylight dances, shadows stretch,
In this realm, our souls connect.

A bridge between two worlds unseen,
In their glow, we find the green.
Luminescence in every heart,
As day and night play their part.

Ancient Voices in the Quiet Grove

In a glade where stillness reigns,
Ancient voices weave through chains.
Whispers low among the trees,
Tales carried by the gentle breeze.

Time stands still where shadows blend,
With every turn, a story penned.
Roots entangle in the earth,
Echoes tracing back to birth.

Mossy stones and weathered bark,
Hold the secrets, light and dark.
In the quiet, wisdom calls,
As the twilight gently falls.

Cloak of night, a velvet sheet,
Wrapped around the forest's feet.
Stars above, like fireflies,
Illuminate the whispered sighs.

Listening close, the heart will learn,
From the grove, where spirits yearn.
In nature's cradle, peace is found,
Ancient voices all around.

Enigmas of the Pine-Wrapped Tranquility

In shadows deep, where silence sings,
The pine trees sway, the owl takes wing.
Amidst the scent of resin's flow,
Mysteries weave, the whispers grow.

Footsteps linger, soft and light,
As secret paths beckon the night.
With every breath, the stillness calls,
In tranquil realms, a magic sprawls.

Veils of fog, like dreams they pass,
Through ancient woods, on emerald grass.
In tranquil hearts, the stories hum,
Of nature's tales, our souls become.

The twilight paints a canvas wide,
Where shadows in the daylight hide.
In pine-wrapped peace, the mind can soar,
Finding answers, seeking more.

In every breeze, a thought entwined,
In hushed repose, the world aligned.
So linger here, where time stands still,
In pine-wrapped calm, you find your will.

Secrets in Shade and Light

Beneath the boughs where light does play,
Soft whispers slide through green array.
Dappled spots where shadows dance,
Invite the heart to take a chance.

The sun, it weaves a golden thread,
As leaves above, in silence, spread.
In secret corners, dreams take flight,
In gentle whispers, shade and light.

Cloaked in green, the stories hide,
In soft embrace, they do confide.
A dance of hues, a symphony,
In every glance, a mystery.

Echoes linger in the air,
Of joyful songs and whispered care.
With every step, the world reveals,
The hidden truths that nature heals.

In twilight's grasp, the secrets bloom,
As shadows stretch, dispelling gloom.
In shade and light, our hearts unite,
Embracing all, both day and night.

Whispers of the Silent Grove

In the grove where silence dwells,
Whispers low like distant bells.
Secrets shared in the gentle breeze,
Among the branches of ancient trees.

Birds take flight, in joyous arcs,
While sunlight breaks, igniting sparks.
Every leaf a tale untold,
In the silence, magic unfolds.

Footprints trace a winding plight,
Where shadows linger, soft and slight.
In every pause, the world aligns,
As whispers dance in tangled vines.

The air is thick with stories old,
Of lovers' vows and dreams retold.
In the quiet, listen well,
For every tree has tales to tell.

In twilight's hush, the stories merge,
As fireflies rise, their flickers surge.
In silent groves, our hearts ignite,
Drawing close to the night's delight.

Harmony Among the Branches

Beneath the branches, harmony sings,
As leaves unite on gentle wings.
In every rustle, a soft refrain,
Nature's symphony, pure and plain.

With sunlit grace, shadows unwind,
In woven paths, our souls aligned.
Birdsong flutters in the air,
Echoing peace, dispelling care.

Roots entwined in sacred ground,
Where every heartbeat can be found.
In quiet moments, stillness reigns,
As nature whispers in soft refrains.

Time stands still, in twilight's glow,
The branches sway, and breezes blow.
Together we find our gentle place,
In nature's arms, a warm embrace.

With every dawn, new dreams awake,
As light pours in, the shadows break.
In harmony, we stand as one,
Among the branches, beneath the sun.

Dialogues of the Dawn Chorus

The sun begins to rise, soft glow,
Birds awaken with a gentle trill,
Whispers of the morning breeze,
Nature's symphony, calm and still.

A robin sings a tale of cheer,
Its notes dance lightly through the air,
The world stirs with a joyful beat,
Awakening dreams beyond compare.

The sparrow chirps, a playful tune,
While dewdrops glitter on the grass,
Each voice a thread in nature's weave,
A chorus welcoming the day at last.

As harmony envelops the sky,
Each creature joins, a vibrant sound,
In this sacred moment shared,
Hope and beauty all around.

With every note that fills the dawn,
Life emerges, fresh and new,
In dialogues of the dawn chorus,
The world awakens, painted in hue.

Recollections of the Forest's Breath

Amid tall trees where shadows play,
The whispers of the leaves invite,
Memories dance on the forest floor,
A tapestry of day and night.

The scent of pine, so rich and deep,
Echoes of laughter, whispers of old,
Sunlight filters through canopies,
Secrets shared in the silence bold.

Crickets serenade the twilight,
While fireflies twinkle, soft and bright,
A symphony of the woodland's breath,
Where time stands still, wrapped in light.

Among the ferns, stories unfold,
Each rustle a page yet to be read,
In the hush, the past reclaims,
The dreams of all who dared to tread.

From roots to boughs, the forest holds,
A myriad tales within its grace,
In recollections of nature's heart,
The essence of life finds its place.

Fragments of Forgotten Tales

In the attic of the mind, they dwell,
Whispers wrapped in dust and dreams,
Fragments of stories long untold,
Glimmers of truth within moonbeams.

A faded book with tattered spine,
Holds echoes of laughter, love, and loss,
Each page a portal to the past,
In shadows where time is embossed.

Forgotten heroes, brave and bold,
Their journeys etched in twilight's haze,
The firelight flickers, revealing paths,
Where memory lingers, a gentle blaze.

Old photographs in sepia tones,
Speak volumes without uttered words,
Each face a chapter, each smile a song,
Life's melody, as soft as birds.

Fragments whisper from the heart,
Inviting us to pause and hear,
In silence, listen to the tales,
Time's gentle muse drawing us near.

Echoed Wishes in the Woodlands

Beneath the boughs of ancient trees,
Wishes flutter like leaves in flight,
Carried softly on the breeze,
A tapestry of hopes ignites.

In moonlit glades, dreams intertwine,
Where starlight weaves a silken thread,
The heart speaks loud, the soul aligns,
With whispered thoughts that never fled.

Echoes of laughter bounce through glens,
Each sound a promise to be kept,
In nature's cradle, where time suspends,
Lies the essence of dreams adept.

Around the brook, wishes unfurl,
Reflections dance on the water's face,
In every ripple, life's joyful swirl,
An invitation to embrace grace.

Beneath the canopy, we find our way,
In echoed wishes from the past,
The woodlands whisper, come what may,
Together, in nature, our hearts held fast.

Echos of the Nature's Poetry

Whispers dance in the green,
Singing songs of the unseen.
Stars above softly gleam,
Nature's voice, a tranquil dream.

Breezes carry tales of old,
In every rustle, secrets told.
Mountains echo with a sigh,
In the shadows, whispers lie.

Rivers flow with rhythmic grace,
Reflecting time, a silent space.
Leaves applaud in gentle cheer,
In this moment, peace is near.

Clouds drift by, a fleeting phase,
Painting skies in softest haze.
Nature's canvas ever bright,
Emerging from the quiet night.

In each sound, a story grows,
In the heart, where silence flows.
Echos weave through every heart,
Unified in nature's art.

Tranquil Tones of the Tall Trees

Gentle giants touch the sky,
Roots that reach, branches high.
In their shade, shadows play,
Whispered secrets drift away.

Leaves will rustle, soft and light,
Telling tales from day to night.
Circles of life intertwined,
Peaceful moments, nature aligned.

Sunlight filters through their crown,
Casting dreams upon the ground.
Breezes carry melodic sound,
A symphony that knows no bound.

Time stands still within their grace,
In their arms, we find our place.
Calm wraps around, a gentle hug,
In the forest, all feel snug.

Each tree holds stories untold,
Of love, loss, and dreams of old.
In their presence, we feel free,
In tranquil tones, the tall trees.

Rhapsody of the Ferns

Ferns unfurl in soft embrace,
Nature's dancers, full of grace.
Emerald green in a bright light,
Whispering secrets, pure delight.

Textures weave beneath the shade,
In each curve, a promise made.
Rustling softly as they sway,
A melody of life at play.

Morning dew, glistening bright,
Wraps the ferns in precious light.
They cradle dreams of earth and time,
In their silence, echoes rhyme.

Shade and sunlight intertwine,
Painting patterns, bold, divine.
In their realm, a tranquil flow,
Ferns sing softly, letting go.

Rhapsody of life they write,
In the forest, pure delight.
Nature's breath in every leaf,
In their presence, find belief.

Tales Woven by the Wind

Whispers drift on gentle gales,
Carrying forth forgotten tales.
Through the valleys, across the plains,
Nature's voice forever reigns.

In the trees, a song resides,
As the wind through branches glides.
Each note carries dreams anew,
In a dance, the world we view.

Clouds that wander, stories bring,
Of distant lands where choirs sing.
In each breeze, a secret shared,
A love for life, forever bared.

Mountains echo with a laugh,
As the wind carves nature's path.
Soft and strong, it knows the way,
Guiding dreams by night and day.

Tales woven in the open air,
Whispered softly, everywhere.
Listen close; the stories blend,
In the whispers, hearts transcend.

A Lantern for the Weary Traveler

In the night, a glow appears,
Guiding hearts through deepened fears.
Its warm embrace calls them near,
A safe haven, crystal clear.

Shadows dance upon the ground,
With every step, the stars astound.
Hope ignites like flickering flame,
A journey forged, no one the same.

Footprints etched in twilight's sigh,
Whispers soft as winds drift by.
Together, we shall find our way,
Until the break of dawn's first ray.

The weary find their strength anew,
As dreams take flight, the path rings true.
With a lantern held, they roam,
To every place they make a home.

So let the light forever shine,
Upon the trails where souls entwine.
In every heart, a beacon bright,
A guiding star through endless night.

Secrets Beneath the Forest Floor

In silence deep, where shadows creep,
The secrets hide, where roots do seep.
Whispers linger, tales untold,
In the earth, a treasure bold.

Mossy blankets keep them warm,
Nature's pulse, a quiet charm.
Fungi dance with colors rare,
Revealing wonders, unaware.

Circles formed by ancient trees,
Rustle softly with the breeze.
Life abounds in every nook,
Hidden paths in every book.

Moonlit nights invite the dreams,
Where moonlight weaves through silver beams.
The forest breathes a solemn sigh,
In harmony, the secrets lie.

Within the roots, the stories flow,
Of times forgotten, lost in woe.
Listen close, the earth's soft lore,
To cherish all that's here and more.

Enchanted by Nature's Palette

Brushstrokes bright on canvas wide,
Nature blooms with colors tied.
Petals dance in morning light,
A painter's dream, a pure delight.

Golden hues of sunlit morn,
Softest whispers, beauty born.
Each leaf sings a melody,
In harmony, they come to be.

Rivers glisten, sapphire streams,
While mountains cradle silver dreams.
The symphony of life resounds,
In every heart, the magic found.

With every step through woods so deep,
The wonders of the world unkeep.
A tapestry of green and blue,
A chorus sung, forever true.

A canvas spread where magic flows,
In every petal, every rose.
Enchanted, lost in nature's grace,
An artist's heart finds its warm place.

Glimpses of Forgotten Whispers

In twilight's hush, the echoes hum,
Of tales long past, the voices come.
Each whisper carries time's embrace,
Reflecting dreams in endless space.

Through shadows thick, the stories weave,
Of hearts that loved, and hearts that grieve.
Each breath a chance to feel the past,
In every moment, shadows cast.

The gentle breeze recalls the lore,
Of laughter spilled on memory's floor.
In every sigh, a fleeting glance,
Of life lived bold, a timeless dance.

Glimpses shine like stars at night,
Guiding the lost with their soft light.
In every corner, whispers grow,
Reminding us of all we know.

So listen close, the echoes call,
A soft reminder weaves through all.
The past and present intertwine,
In whispers sweet, forever shine.

Nature's Softest Whispers

In the glade where wildflowers grow,
The gentle breeze begins to blow.
Birds chirp softly, their songs a treat,
Nature's heart, a rhythmic beat.

Sunlight dances on leaves so green,
In this haven, peace is seen.
Softly rustling, the tall grass sways,
Whispers of nature fill the days.

Clouds drift lazily in the sky,
While butterflies flit gently by.
Life unfolds in colors bright,
A canvas woven with pure delight.

Mountains stand with dignity tall,
A silent witness to it all.
In valleys deep, where rivers flow,
Nature's magic, a soft glow.

Each moment fleeting, yet so grand,
A miracle crafted by nature's hand.
In this world of peace and grace,
We find our hearts, our rightful place.

The Symphony of Boughs

Underneath the arching trees,
An orchestra plays with the breeze.
Woodwinds rustle, strings that creak,
Nature's concert, serene and sleek.

Leaves whisper tales of days gone by,
As squirrels leap and birds cry.
The sunlight filters through the bark,
Creating music in the dark.

Branches sway in a gentle dance,
Nature's rhythm, a fleeting chance.
With every rustle, every sigh,
The symphony reaches for the sky.

The earth hums a grounded tune,
Beneath the watchful eye of the moon.
From the roots up to the crown,
Nature's voice, a timeless sound.

As night descends, the melody fades,
Yet still, the magic never evades.
The symphony lives in silent night,
In every shadow, every light.

Shadows in the Sunlight

Beneath the trees, shadows play,
A dance of light throughout the day.
Softly cast, each shape a tale,
In sunlit warmth, where whispers sail.

Children laugh, as time stands still,
Chasing shadows, hearts to fill.
The world a canvas, bright and bold,
With each shadow, a story told.

Petals fall in a gentle breeze,
While sunbeams filter through the leaves.
Nature paints in hues of gold,
A masterpiece both new and old.

Pathways winding, soft beneath,
Life's vibrant tapestry, a wreath.
In every corner, joy abounds,
In sunlight's grasp, true love surrounds.

As daylight wanes, the shadows grow,
With twilight's kiss, the magic flows.
In every heart, a memory stays,
Shadows in sunlight, all our days.

Hushed Conversations of the Trees

In quiet woods, the trees confide,
Their secrets held, their roots entwined.
Whispered tales of storms and sun,
In hushed tones, their stories run.

Leaves debate in a soft rustle,
While acorns drop, the earth to tussle.
In the stillness, wisdom flows,
A thousand years in every pose.

Branches sway with gentle grace,
Each movement, a sacred space.
In every creak, a lifetime's sigh,
The trees stand tall, as ages fly.

Fragrant pine and sturdy oak,
In unity, their voices spoke.
Their silent language, rich and deep,
Awakens dreams from peaceful sleep.

When night descends, their talks still bloom,
Underneath the starry gloom.
Together, they embrace the night,
Hushed conversations, pure delight.

Secrets of the Pine-Infused Air

Whispers dance in the twilight,
Secrets linger in the breeze.
Pine needles carpet the forest floor,
Memories held in ancient trees.

Each breath whispers tales untold,
Of nature's heart, both fierce and mild.
The scent of earth and pine entwined,
Wraps the spirit like a child.

From shadows deep, the past emerges,
Beneath the boughs, a world unfurls.
Life cycles spin in intricate threads,
Nature's magic swirls and twirls.

A soft breeze brings the warmth of sun,
And echoes through the fragrant wood.
Nature's secrets, forever spun,
Hope and peace at every flood.

Here in the stillness, dreams arise,
Borne on the wind, where moments share.
In pine-infused air, a sweet surprise,
Our hearts lay bare, without a care.

Symphonies in the Sylvan

The forest sings in vibrant tones,
A symphony of rustling leaves.
Birds chirp melodies of the morn,
While sunlight filters through the eaves.

Each step reveals a rhythmic pulse,
Nature's heartbeat, strong and true.
The babbling brook joins in the song,
A harmony that pulls us through.

In the embrace of ancient trees,
We find a peace, a place to roam.
The whispers of the sylvan world,
Call us back to nature's home.

Underneath the vaulted sky,
The stars align with forest's thrall.
Symphonies interlace and blend,
Echoing the heart's sweet call.

As twilight drapes its velvet cloak,
The orchestra of night takes lead.
Each note a dream, each sound a hope,
A timeless gift we all may heed.

Dreams of the Canopy's Embrace

High above the world below,
The canopy of dreams unfolds.
Branches weave a gentle cradle,
Each leaf a story yet untold.

Sunlight filters through the gaps,
Creating patterns, light and shade.
A haven of tranquility,
Where moments linger, softly made.

Birds flit through a tranquil sea,
Their songs like whispers in the air.
Nestled in the arms of green,
We find a peace beyond compare.

As shadows lengthen with the dusk,
The forest sighs, a softened breath.
The dreams of trees, both old and wise,
Remind us of life, love, and death.

In the embrace of leafy heights,
Our spirits dance, wild and free.
In this realm of dreams untamed,
We breathe in what it means to be.

Stories Beneath the Starlit Boughs

Underneath the starry skies,
Whispers float with secrets old.
Beneath the branches, stories lie,
In moonlit silver, softly told.

The nightingale sings to the moon,
Her melody weaves tales so bright.
Each twinkling star a beacon clear,
Guides wanderers through the night.

Crickets join in, their chorus strong,
A symphony beneath the boughs.
Each shadow dances, plays along,
As nature takes a sacred vow.

In this realm where silence reigns,
The world outside is far away.
We lose ourselves in whispered dreams,
Awash in night's enchanting sway.

Here, where every branch is wise,
And stories are boundless as the sea,
We gather under starlit skies,
Embraced by nature's mystery.

Tranquil Echoes of Time

Whispers of ages in the breeze,
Softly they carry ancient tales,
Ripples of moments, frozen ease,
In twilight's embrace, the heart exhales.

Fading shadows dance on the floor,
As stars begin to softly gleam,
Time's gentle pulse, forevermore,
Guides us through a waking dream.

Silence unfolds in golden light,
A tapestry woven with care,
Where memories linger, pure delight,
And every heartbeat, vast and rare.

Echoes of laughter, sweet and kind,
Enfolded in the arms of peace,
With every moment, we unwind,
Each memory, a cherished fleece.

In the stillness, wisdom grows,
As hours slip through tender hands,
Tranquil echoes, softly flows,
Time's embrace, where stillness stands.

Painter of Dappled Light

Brush in hand, a soul takes flight,
Colors swirl in sunlit streams,
Crafting visions bold and bright,
A canvas woven from sweet dreams.

Whispers painted on the air,
Each stroke a story to reveal,
Nature's palette, rich and rare,
Unfolds the magic we can feel.

Dappled light through leaves above,
Creates a symphony of glade,
A serenade of peace and love,
In every hue, the heart is swayed.

Every sunset, gold to rose,
Brushes blend in soft embrace,
While quiet night begins to close,
The stars appear, a jeweled lace.

For life is art, an endless quest,
To find the beauty in the day,
As colors mingle, hearts are blessed,
A painter's world, forever play.

The Stillness Between Seasons

Leaves whisper secrets to the ground,
As autumn fades to winter's hold,
In silent moments, peace is found,
A tapestry of dust and gold.

Frost-kissed air, a breath divine,
The world transforms, yet still remains,
Nature's pulse, a gentle line,
Binding time with soft refrains.

Buds of spring await their turn,
A promise held in quiet grace,
While hearts in silent yearning burn,
Yearning for warmth in nature's face.

Between the softest breaths we stand,
In sacred pause, a tranquil space,
Life's whispered dreams, a gentle hand,
In each season, we find our place.

From winter's hush to summer's song,
The stillness weaves its gentle thread,
Time marches forth, yet here we long,
To cherish all that lies ahead.

Beneath a Canopy of Dreams

Branches weave a soft embrace,
Where shadows dance in filtered light,
Beneath the leaves, a sacred space,
Where whispers float into the night.

Stars peek through in twinkling eyes,
As crickets sing a lullaby,
A world awakened, yet it lies,
In harmony, it breathes a sigh.

In this haven, fears dissolve,
Each moment wraps us, pure and free,
As woven dreams begin to evolve,
A tapestry of you and me.

The air is filled with magic's kiss,
As time slows down, our hearts align,
In twilight's glow, we find our bliss,
A dance of souls, where love can shine.

Beneath this vault of starlit chrome,
We share our hopes, our wildest schemes,
In every breath, we find a home,
Awake, together, in our dreams.

Murmurs Among the Needles

Whispers weave through branches high,
Softly spoken, a secret sigh.
Gentle rustle, nature's tune,
Echoes linger 'neath the moon.

Light filters through in golden beams,
Casting shadows on woodland dreams.
Murmurs blend with the breath of leaves,
A serenade that never leaves.

Each step dances on pine's embrace,
Time slows down, a tender space.
In harmony, the forest sings,
Painting peace with gentle wings.

The breeze carries tales of yore,
Of ancient roots and forest lore.
Murmurs drift on the cool night air,
In every whisper, love laid bare.

Dance of the Pine Cones

Pine cones tumble, a playful dance,
Spinning, twirling, in nature's glance.
Among the needles, they take flight,
In the soft embrace of fading light.

Chasing shadows, the wind does sway,
Each cone a partner in forest ballet.
They gather round the towering trees,
Whirling softly, carried by the breeze.

A symphony of rustling sounds,
Echoing softly in the mounds.
They spin in circles, laughter's song,
Unity found where they all belong.

With every motion, stories told,
Of seasons changing, trees growing bold.
Caught in the magic of twilight's grace,
The dance of life in this sacred space.

Solitude in the Forest's Heart

In the quiet, whispers fade,
Where shadows dance in cool cascade.
A lone traveler wanders deep,
In nature's arms, away from sleep.

Among the ferns, a secret place,
Time stands still, a gentle pace.
The trees embrace, a calming breath,
Within the stillness, life and death.

Soft overhanging canopies sway,
As sunlight filters through the gray.
Each step a rhythm, the heart's own beat,
In solitude, life feels complete.

Echoes linger in the air,
Every moment a tender prayer.
Here in the forest, peace resides,
In silence deep, the spirit glides.

Breath of the Evergreen

Evergreen whispers in the breeze,
Swaying gently among the trees.
A fragrant sigh of life anew,
In every breath, the world feels true.

Beneath the canopy so vast,
Time slows down, the die is cast.
Branches stretching, reaching wide,
Nature's pulse, a tranquil guide.

Golden sunlight, dappled glow,
Kissing trunks in a soft flow.
A moment captured under sky,
As whispers dance, and dreams fly high.

In the echo, a love profound,
Among the evergreens, peace is found.
Each breath a promise of the night,
In the forest's heart, all feels right.

Shades of Solitude Beneath the Pines

In the quiet grove, shadows play,
Whispers of nature drift away.
Lonely thoughts in the soft light dwell,
Each moment here a calming spell.

Rustling needles, the pine trees sigh,
Beneath their arms, my spirits fly.
Nature's embrace, a gentle friend,
In solitude, I find my mend.

Time meanders, soft and slow,
Where wildflowers and secrets grow.
Above, the clouds weave stories bright,
In shadows deep, I claim my right.

The breeze carries a subtle tune,
A melody soft as afternoon.
With each breath, the moment stays,
Lost in the magic of these days.

Under pines, the world's a blur,
Every worry starts to stir.
Yet here, with peace, I shall remain,
Beneath the pines, I feel no pain.

Fables Shared in the Shade

In the dappled light, stories unfold,
Whispers of legends, age-old and bold.
Beneath the leaves, tales come alive,
In gentle shades, imaginations thrive.

A fox shares wisdom, sly and bright,
While turtles teach of patience and flight.
The old oak nods with knowing grace,
As sunbeams dance in this sacred space.

In the hush where dreams take flight,
Creatures gather, heartening the night.
A rabbit sings of the morrow's quest,
While crickets chirp in a rhythmic fest.

Among the fables, laughter grows,
As nature's chorus softly flows.
Moments cherished in the glen,
These precious tales we share again.

Echoes linger long after dusk,
Each story wrapped in fragrant husk.
In the shade, our spirits soar,
Fables shared forevermore.

Chants of the Woodland Breeze

Listen closely, hear the sound,
Chants of breezes swirling around.
Each rustle whispers, soft and clear,
Nature's hymn, a song sincere.

Through the branches, voices weave,
Carrying tales the trees believe.
A gentle murmur, sweet and low,
In the woods where secrets flow.

The leaves applaud in rhythmic sway,
As twilight opens up the day.
With every gulp of evening's sigh,
The woodland breathes, the spirits fly.

Every sigh a story shared,
In the dusky light, we're ensnared.
Echoing laughter, the night's embrace,
In the woodland's heart, we find our place.

Chants of the breeze, soft and bright,
Guide us through the velvet night.
Lost in nature, forever free,
In this symphony, you and me.

Behind the Bark and Branch

Behind the bark, the stories hide,
Secrets woven, nature's pride.
Each branch a witness, sturdy and spare,
To all the lives that linger there.

A flicker of movement, a whispering breeze,
Life unfolds among the trees.
The sap that flows, both thick and sweet,
Bears the history beneath our feet.

In gnarled roots, the past is found,
Echoes of footsteps on the ground.
The stories linger, rich and vast,
With every heartbeat, shadows cast.

Underneath the canopy's shade,
Memories dance while spirits wade.
In this stillness, time stands still,
Behind the bark, I find my will.

Nature's library, pages turned,
With every glance, a lesson learned.
Behind the bark, a world awaits,
A life of wonder that resonates.

Beneath the Canopy

Beneath the canopy of green,
Whispers of nature can be seen.
Leaves dance gently in the air,
As sunlight filters everywhere.

Mossy carpets underfoot,
Softly cradle every root.
Squirrels chatter, birds will sing,
Calling out for early spring.

In this realm of peace and light,
Creatures dart and take to flight.
Time slows down; the world grows still,
In the woods, our hearts will fill.

Branches sway with tales untold,
Secrets held in bark and fold.
Every step with wonder brings,
Beneath the canopy of things.

Secrets of the Woodland Breeze

Through the trees, a breeze does weave,
Carrying whispers we believe.
Rustling leaves with stories old,
Of ancient paths and dreams retold.

The sun dips low; shadows play,
On the forest floor, they lay.
Each soft sigh from nature's heart,
Brings us close, though we're apart.

The ferns grow lush, the brambles thick,
Nature's magic, swift and quick.
In every gust, a secret breathes,
The whispering dance of woodland leaves.

Mysteries in every glance,
An invitation, a sweet chance.
To linger still and feel the peace,
In the quiet, life's release.

Songs of the Sylvan Shadows

In the shadows where tales reside,
Nature's secrets softly hide.
Silhouettes in twilight glow,
Sing of wonders we don't know.

Gentle winds carry the tune,
Underneath the silver moon.
Branches sway, a rhythmic play,
Echoing the dreams of day.

Crickets chirp in harmony,
A serenade so wild and free.
The forest breathes, in every sigh,
Songs of sylvan shadows fly.

Through the night, a symphony,
Nature's voice, our melody.
In the hush, we hear the call,
Of the shadows, inviting all.

Echoes of the Tall Sentinels

Tall sentinels stand proud and wide,
Guardians of the forest's stride.
Wood and bark, a weathered skin,
Holding tales of where we've been.

They reach towards the skies above,
Whispering stories, hope, and love.
Each ring a memory, each knot a tale,
Through storm and sun, they will not frail.

Echoes linger in the air,
Of laughter, joy, and silent prayer.
As branches arc in twilight's glow,
Their wisdom flows, a steady flow.

In the stillness, hear the sound,
Of every promise, all around.
Sentinels of time, they stand,
Guardians of this sacred land.

Sonorous Secrets of the Swaying Trees

Whispers dance upon the breeze,
Leaves are murmuring ancient pleas.
Roots entwined with tales untold,
In every branch, a secret bold.

Twilight fades to twilight's song,
Nature's chorus, sweet and strong.
Boughs embrace the evening light,
Guardians of the coming night.

In shadows deep, the stories weave,
Rustling tales for those who cleave.
Branches bow to welcome dreams,
In their sway, hope gently gleams.

Underneath the vast expanse,
Nature's heart begins to dance.
Beacons of the wild unfold,
Swaying softly, secrets told.

As the stars begin to sing,
Branches sway, the night they bring.
In this realm of whispering trees,
Solace found in nature's breeze.

Mysteries of the Wooded Realm

Beneath the canopies so high,
Ancient stories linger nigh.
Footsteps light on mossy floor,
Nature's secrets to explore.

Misty mornings veil the ground,
In stillness, echoes softly sound.
Animals stir, shadows play,
As dawn breaks bright the new day.

In twilight's grasp, the woods conspire,
To weave enchantments, never tire.
With every rustle, every sigh,
An ancient wisdom whispers by.

Ferns unfurl with gentle grace,
Inviting all to slow the pace.
Each path a journey, wild and free,
Unlock the mysteries, just be.

In the heart of the wooded land,
Magic rests within the hand.
Nature's book, a tale unknown,
In every leaf, a truth is sown.

Voices Cradled by the Pines

High above, the pines do sway,
Holding whispers day by day.
Gentle sighs in twilight's glow,
Cradled secrets, soft and low.

In the stillness, hearts align,
Echoed dreams where shadows shine.
Among the trunks, a song is spun,
Of moments lost and battles won.

Underneath their watchful gaze,
Time unfolds in quiet ways.
The needles drop, a soft embrace,
Nature's love, a sacred space.

As dusk descends, the world slows down,
Nature wears its velvet crown.
In the pines, a lullaby,
Hearts find peace as eagles fly.

A forest deep with stories grand,
Wrapped in love, a gentle hand.
Voices cradled, soft and serene,
In the pines, a timeless dream.

Chronicles of Nature's Quiet

Softly speaks the morning dew,
In whispers clear and so true.
Every petal, every stone,
Holds a story of its own.

In the hush, the moments pause,
Nature's breath, a gentle cause.
Quiet streams with silver gleams,
Flowing silently through dreams.

Underneath the starlit sky,
Each heartbeat bids the world goodbye.
In the stillness, souls align,
Finding grace in every sign.

Winds of change through branches sweep,
Carrying secrets we keep.
With every rustle, soft and light,
Chronicles of nature's night.

Wait unto the dawn's latest birth,
In the quiet, we find our worth.
Nature's stories, profound and vast,
In the silence, they hold fast.

Tread Lightly

Tread lightly upon the ground,
Whispers of nature all around.
Each step a note, a gentle sound,
In this sacred space, we're earthbound.

The trees sway, dance in the breeze,
Guardians of secrets, they never cease.
With every rustle, they share their peace,
In a world where worries can release.

Sunlight trickles through the leaves,
Nature's tapestry, it weaves.
Take a moment, the heart believes,
In the magic that it conceives.

Listen closely, hear the call,
Of the forest, who welcomes all.
A symphony in shadows tall,
In unity, we stand enthralled.

So tread lightly, share the grace,
Leave no mark, let love embrace.
In this haven, find your place,
Together, humanity and nature's face.

The Forest Listens

In the hush of evening light,
The forest holds its breath so tight.
Every creature, every sight,
Turns to listen, day turns night.

Leaves murmur tales of old,
Stories of warmth, of hearts bold.
Winds carry secrets, soft and cold,
The forest listens, silent and gold.

A rustle here, a whisper there,
Echoing love, sadness, despair.
In the thicket, the heart laid bare,
The forest sighs, a soothing prayer.

Branches weave a mystic verse,
Connecting the cosmos, unbound by curse.
In vibrant notes, they softly disperse,
The forest listens, a universe.

So pause awhile, breathe the air,
In the woods, find solace rare.
Feel the pulse, the love laid bare,
For the forest listens, with tender care.

Song of the Sylvan Spirits

In twilight's glow, they take their flight,
Sylvan spirits, pure delight.
Through the canopy, they ignite,
A song of joy, echoes of night.

With each flutter, leaves will sway,
Nature's chorus, come what may.
In harmony, they gently play,
Whispers of hope, a bright array.

Dancing shadows, glimmers bright,
In the heart of the soft moonlight.
Every note, a spark of sight,
A lullaby that feels so right.

Feel the rhythm, the earth's embrace,
In every corner, every space.
With each heartbeat, we find our place,
In the song of spirits, lost in grace.

Let the melody guide your soul,
In nature's arms, we become whole.
With sylvan spirits, we are one goal,
A timeless tune, love's gentle roll.

Emotions Wrapped in Pine Needles

Softly falling, pine needles rest,
A blanket woven, nature's best.
Whispers cradle the weary chest,
Each layer speaks, emotions blessed.

In the scent of earth, we find peace,
A refuge where troubles cease.
Wrapped in green, the heart's release,
Pine needles hold our joys, increase.

Secrets linger in every tree,
Soft echoes of you and me.
In nature's arms, we feel so free,
Emotions flow, so gracefully.

Gather moments, gentle and kind,
In this sanctuary, peace we find.
Each pine needle, a thought aligned,
A tapestry of hearts entwined.

So walk the path through winding trails,
Where love and grace never pales.
Wrapped in whispers of pine scales,
In emotions strong, our spirit sails.

The Solitary Path of Green

A winding path, so lush and bright,
The solitary way feels right.
With every step, the heart takes flight,
In the embrace of nature's light.

Surrounded by a sea of trees,
Whispers carried on the breeze.
In solitude, the spirit sees,
The beauty found in simple pleas.

Each leaf a mirror, reflecting dreams,
The path uncovers silent themes.
Nature hugs, while sunlight beams,
A journey blessed, so real it seems.

Footsteps echo, soft and slow,
In this green haven, hearts will grow.
The world outside, we gently forego,
On the solitary path, we know.

So wander forth, let silence sing,
In every moment, joy will bring.
The solitary path of green,
Is where our hearts find everything.

Reflections in the Pine's Shade

Beneath the pine, shadows sway,
Whispers of a gentle day.
Softly the needles, they dance and play,
Nature's breath, in lush array.

A mirror of green, the forest glows,
With each breeze, the silence grows.
Time stands still where the cool wind blows,
In this haven, peace bestows.

Crickets sing in evening's light,
Echoing dreams, taking flight.
Underneath stars, a serene sight,
Holding night in soft twilight.

Reflections deep as rivers run,
Every moment slips like sun.
In the pine's shade, life's begun,
A symphony, weaves as one.

Here, a solitude embraced,
In the pine's arms, fears erased.
With each heartbeat, time is chased,
In Nature's love, forever placed.

Whispers of Old Growth

In the depths where giants stand,
Heartbeats pulse through the land.
Whispers float on breezes planned,
Stories of time, forever grand.

Moss carpets the timbers old,
Each creak sings tales untold.
Leaves in bloom, a greenfold,
Secrets of life softly scrolled.

Sunlight dapples through the leaves,
Nature's wisdom gently weaves.
The coolness of shade deceives,
Where even the weary believes.

A refuge for those who roam,
Finding solace, calling home.
In the embrace of nature's dome,
The forest sings a timeless poem.

Echoes linger in the air,
With history's weight, they share.
In old growth, we find repair,
A sacred bond, beyond compare.

Shade and Shadow in Quietude

In the glade where shadows lie,
Quietude whispers, soft and spry.
Under the leaves, dreams drift high,
Nature's cradle, a gentle sigh.

Cool earth welcomes every being,
In this silence, lives are seeing.
Moments cherished, softly freeing,
Hearts entwined in quiet agreeing.

Branches arch like arms in prayer,
A sanctuary beyond compare.
In the shade, worries laid bare,
Finding calm in the still air.

Light flickers, a dance of grace,
Nature's rhythm finds its place.
In the hush, we slow the chase,
Learning love in this embrace.

Every rustle tells a tale,
Of fleeting moments, soft and frail.
Breath of life in the forest's veil,
In shade and shadow, we prevail.

The Language of the Forest Floor

Upon the ground, a world unseen,
Whispers echo where leaves convene.
Roots entwined, in earth, they glean,
The language spoken, evergreen.

Mushrooms sprout in quiet grace,
Fungi's touch, a soft embrace.
Nature's pen in the still space,
Stories etched, time cannot erase.

The crunch of twigs beneath our feet,
In every step, life's heartbeat.
Pebbles gleam where shadows meet,
In the forest's dance, we retreat.

Nature's canvas, painted bold,
With secrets waiting to be told.
In the underbrush, life unfolds,
A silent wisdom made of gold.

Listen closely, to the ground,
In the whispers, wonder's found.
From the soil, connections bound,
In the forest's heart, we are crowned.

A Tale Woven in Green

In the forest deep, where whispers flow,
A tapestry of leaves begins to glow.
Every step a story, every bough a dream,
Nature's gentle hand weaves a silver seam.

Sunlight dances through the emerald shade,
Footfalls echo softly, undeterred, unafraid.
Each flower a chapter, each rock a verse,
In the tale of the wild, we forever immerse.

The brook sings a ballad, crisp and clear,
While creatures of the wood gather near.
Together in harmony, life thrives anew,
In this woven expanse of green and blue.

Seasons change the plot, in colors bright,
From vibrant blooms to the calming night.
Yet every leaf holds whispers of the past,
A tale woven in green, forever steadfast.

So wander this path, let it take you far,
Where the heart finds solace, beneath the stars.
In nature's embrace, let your spirit be free,
For in every rustle, there's a story to see.

Pine-Scented Reveries

Beneath the pines, where shadows play,
A fragrant breeze takes the cares away.
Needles crunch softly underfoot, so sweet,
In this wooded haven, the soul finds its beat.

Golden rays trickle through branches high,
Painting the forest with a warm, gentle sigh.
Every scent a memory, every gust a song,
In the embrace of pines, nothing feels wrong.

The mountains stand guard in their silent grace,
While time drifts slowly in this sacred space.
A symphony of nature, a lullaby grand,
In pine-scented dreams, we forever stand.

Clouds weave through treetops, light and free,
Casting soft shadows, a playful decree.
The world fades away, just moments remain,
In this fragrant retreat, no hint of disdain.

So breathe in deep, let the essence surround,
In the scented reveries, peace can be found.
Underneath the pines, let your worries cease,
For here in the stillness, discover your peace.

Embrace of the Great Outdoors

Where mountains rise and rivers weave,
The great outdoors beckons, ready to leave.
With open arms, it calls us near,
In this wild embrace, we shed all fear.

Fields of wildflowers burst into bloom,
Painting the landscape with nature's perfume.
The sun kisses earth with a golden hue,
In this vibrant realm, our spirits renew.

Soft whispers of wind through trees overhead,
A song of adventure, where dreams are fed.
Climb every summit, feel the air so pure,
In the embrace of the wild, we shall endure.

Stars blanket the sky, twinkling bright,
Night wraps us gently in its soothing light.
Every heartbeat echoes in the wide expanse,
In nature's arms, we take our chance.

So venture forth with courage anew,
In the great outdoors, find the path that's true.
Let the mountains and rivers chart your course,
For in nature's embrace, we feel life's force.

Shrouded in Verdancy

In the hush of the grove, where shadows blend,
A veil of verdancy begins to descend.
Moss carpets the ground, a soft, gentle bed,
Whispers of secrets that the ancients said.

The canopy dances, a tapestry fair,
With beams of sunlight peeking through air.
Every leaf glistens, kissed by the dew,
In this shrouded haven, life starts anew.

Time flows like water, slow and serene,
In every green corner, a story unseen.
The call of the wild, a soft, beckoning tune,
In the embrace of the leaves, we find our commune.

Creatures dart swiftly, shadows in lace,
Nature's own theater, a mesmerizing space.
With each gentle rustle, spirits begin,
In this verdant cocoon, we find where we've been.

So let the green sanctum hold you tight,
In its lush verdancy, everything feels right.
For wrapped in this beauty, heart and mind blend,
In the dream of the wild, where worries suspend.

Serenity in Shadows and Light

In whispers soft, the shadows weave,
Their gentle dance, a calm reprieve.
Through branches swaying, light will spill,
A tranquil heart, a peaceful will.

The sun dips low; the day takes flight,
Embraced in warm, embracing light.
Each moment held in silent grace,
A fleeting glimpse, a soft embrace.

The night unfolds, a velvet sheet,
Where dreams and stars in silence meet.
In stillness wrapped, the world will sigh,
As shadows linger, time floats by.

The dance of dusk, a subtle tune,
Awakes the night beneath the moon.
In every flicker, calm takes hold,
A tapestry of stories told.

With every breath, serenity calls,
In shadows deep and light's soft thralls.
A balance struck in nature's play,
Embracing peace at close of day.

Nature's Lullaby in the Pines

Softly whispers, breezes sigh,
Among the pines, where dreams can fly.
The rustling needles, gentle sound,
In nature's arms, our solace found.

The sun peeks through the emerald veil,
A golden hue where shadows trail.
Each branch a cradle, strong and true,
A lullaby of calm and dew.

In every owl's call, a tale unfolds,
While evening wraps the world in gold.
With every step on mossy ground,
The heartbeat of the earth resounds.

The stars above begin to gleam,
A canvas painted with a dream.
In every breath, the wild sings sweet,
A melody where hearts can meet.

Rest now, dear soul, let troubles cease,
In the forest's hug, discover peace.
Nature's lullaby softly plays,
As time drifts slowly, lost in praise.

Stories Carried by the Wind

The wind whispers tales from afar,
From mountain tops to where dreams are.
It carries secrets, old and wise,
Painting stories across the skies.

With every gust, a new refrain,
Echoes of joy, and hints of pain.
Through fields of green and oceans wide,
The windswept tales take flight with pride.

Softly sighing, the breezes tell,
Of forgotten paths, where shadows dwell.
They swirl through trees, a dance of grace,
Each memory wrapped in time and space.

In the rustling leaves, the whispers flow,
Of ancient lands and rivers' glow.
The stories weave, like threads of gold,
In every heart, their magic hold.

Let the gentle breeze your spirit lift,
As it carries onward, a timeless gift.
Through every echo, the stories blend,
In nature's breath, our souls transcend.

The Treetop's Silent Vigil

High above where eagles soar,
The treetops stand, a timeless lore.
In quiet strength, they watch and wait,
Guardians of dreams, they contemplate.

Through storms that rage and skies so blue,
Their branches sway, enduring too.
With whispers soft, they greet the dawn,
Embracing mysteries of the morn.

They hold the tales of seasons past,
In every ring, the memories cast.
A silent vigil, though winds may howl,
Against the time, they silently growl.

The sun will rise, the shadows fade,
In nature's heart, their strength displayed.
With roots that delve in earth so deep,
Promising life, while others sleep.

In twilight's glow, they stand so proud,
The treetop's watch, a vigil loud.
A testament to time's embrace,
In every leaf, a sacred space.

Breath of the Tall Sentinels

Amidst the heights, they stand so proud,
Guardians of dreams, under the cloud.
Whispers of wind through branches flow,
Tales of the ancients, soft and slow.

Roots deep in earth, they grasp the time,
Their stories woven like rhythm and rhyme.
Nature's pillars, strong and true,
Breath of the tall, they nurture too.

In twilight's glow, they sway and bend,
Silhouettes dancing, their shadows blend.
The sky turns pink, a canvas wide,
While secrets dwell in their boughs and side.

Seasonal blooms, a vibrant show,
With autumn's kiss, their colors glow.
Winter's cloak wraps them tight,
Yet life awakens with spring's first light.

So let us gather beneath their grace,
Finding peace in their embrace.
For in their presence, the world feels right,
The breath of sentinels, day and night.

Serenade of the Needle-Laden Branches

In the forest deep, where silence sings,
Needles whisper tales of gentle springs.
The breeze, a bard, strums melodies sweet,
On needle-laden branches, a rhythmic beat.

Dappled sunlight breaks through the green,
Old growths dance, a serene scene.
Rustling softly, the pine trees sway,
Harmonious notes greet the day.

Each needle sharp, yet soothing too,
A carpet of green, a tranquil view.
Echoes of nature blend and twine,
A serenade crafted by design.

With every gust, a song is spun,
Under the gaze of the watchful sun.
Life among the branches takes its flight,
Comfort found in nature's light.

So listen close to the forest's song,
Feel the magic, where we belong.
Needle-laden branches, reach so high,
In their embrace, let worries fly.

Whispers in the Woodland

In shaded glades where shadows play,
Whispers float on the breeze's sway.
Beneath the canopy, secrets dwell,
Nature's chorus, a beautiful spell.

Gentle rustle of leaves above,
Songs of the meadow, tales of love.
Moss-covered stones and trees so grand,
Life entwined in this enchanted land.

Crickets chirp as daylight fades,
Night unveils its velvet shades.
Stars emerge to join the dance,
Whispers echo, a soft romance.

Moonlight bathes the earth in glow,
Night's embrace, a tender show.
Creatures scurry, the world alive,
In the woodland's heart, we thrive.

So pause awhile, let silence breathe,
In whispers, magic weaves beneath.
For in these woods, we find our way,
A tapestry of night and day.

Lullaby of the Leafy Giants

Above the world, they stretch and sway,
Leafy giants watch the day.
With branches wide, they cradle dreams,
In softest whispers, their comfort beams.

Under their watch, the children play,
In laughter bright, they find their way.
Roots entwined in the rich, dark earth,
Silent witnesses to life's birth.

In summer's heat, their shade provides,
Guardians of secrets where stillness hides.
Through winters cold, they remain strong,
A lullaby soft, a timeless song.

When autumn comes, their colors blaze,
Crimson, gold in a splendid phase.
Falling leaves, a gentle plight,
Dance upon the wind's soft flight.

So find a spot beneath their dome,
Feel their presence, a sense of home.
For in their arms, we learn to dream,
Leafy giants, under moonlight's gleam.

Enchanted Conversations of the Green

In the shade where whispers start,
Leaves converse, a gentle art.
Butterflies weave through sunlit beams,
Nature hums its secret dreams.

Mossy carpets cradle feet,
Echoes of the wild heartbeat.
Branches sway in rhythmic rhyme,
A dance of life beyond all time.

Softly spoken, the breeze relays,
Tales of olden, wondrous days.
Each rustle brings a story new,
Enchanting all who sit and view.

Beneath the boughs, we find our place,
In this realm of green embrace.
Voices mingle, blend, and curl,
In enchanted dance, the forest twirls.

Here in whispers, the heart can soar,
In every leaf, a sacred lore.
Nature's chorus, wild and free,
Calls us home, eternally.

Moments Stilled in the Canopy

Glimmers of light through leafy shrouds,
Time stands still amidst thick crowds.
Dappled shadows paint the ground,
In this silence, peace is found.

Birdsong floats on gentle air,
Echoes dance without a care.
Rustle of wings, a soft caress,
Nature's spell, a sweet duress.

Branches cradling morning dew,
Each drop holds a world anew.
Moments captured, fleeting, gone,
In the thrum of life, we yawn.

Whispers linger, secrets shared,
In the canopy, we are bared.
Hearts align with nature's beat,
In stillness, all our souls can meet.

The sun dips low, horizons blaze,
In twilight's breath, a soft amaze.
Captured here, we find our way,
In moments stilled, we choose to stay.

The Song of the Silent Tall Ones

Whispers dwell in forest high,
Where the silent giants lie.
Every trunk a tale retells,
In their midst, our spirit swells.

Leaves like fingers brush the sky,
Branches reach, as if to fly.
In their shade, we pause and sigh,
Seeking solace, asking why.

Raindrops fall with soft embrace,
Nature's pulse, a gentle pace.
The song swells, a melody,
Of life that flows, eternally.

Voices of the past reside,
In each ripple, they abide.
Silent tall ones, wise and free,
Guide our hearts to harmony.

Their roots entwine, a bond of trust,
In time's embrace, we shift to dust.
Yet in their song, we still remain,
A part of nature's grand refrain.

Where Pine Needles Dance

Amidst the pines, a rhythm sways,
In the breeze, where nature plays.
Needles shed in twirling flight,
Softly fall, a lovely sight.

Sunlight dapples through the green,
Nature's canvas, serene sheen.
Every rustle sings a song,
In this place, we all belong.

Wild scents mingle in the air,
Whispers echo, soft and rare.
Footfalls light on needle beds,
Where secrets dwell and magic spreads.

Clouds drift by, a gentle guide,
In the pines, we will abide.
With every breath, we feel alive,
Among the trees, our spirits thrive.

Here, beneath the towering trees,
Moments linger with the breeze.
Where pine needles dance and sway,
In nature's arms, we wish to stay.

Memory of the Whispering Woods

In the grove where shadows play,
Echoes linger, soft and gray.
Leaves whisper secrets of the past,
Time moves slowly, memories cast.

Old trunks stand in silent grace,
Guarding stories in their space.
Footsteps trace the winding trails,
Nature's calm, where heart prevails.

Moonlight dances on the streams,
Carrying whispers of lost dreams.
Through the mist, the feelings sway,
In the woods, forever stay.

Branches reach for starlit skies,
In their shadows, nature sighs.
Each rustle speaks of days gone by,
In the woods, where echoes lie.

Here, we pause and breathe the air,
Find the solace hidden there.
Memory wraps us like a cloak,
In the woods, our hearts have spoke.

Lanterns of the Dusk-lit Pines

In the twilight, lanterns glow,
Casting warmth on paths we know.
Beneath the pines, with gentle light,
We wander softly into night.

Each flicker holds a story told,
Of whispered dreams and hearts of gold.
The breeze carries a sweet refrain,
Like music flowing through the grain.

With every step, the shadows sway,
Guiding us along the way.
The pines stand tall, a watchful crowd,
Veiled in twilight, dreams allowed.

Stars awaken, one by one,
As the day retreats and is done.
The lanterns lead our hearts in dance,
In this magic, take a chance.

Lost in wonder, time does fade,
In the dusk, our fears cascade.
With every glow, we find our part,
In the pines, we share our heart.

Fragrance of the Hidden Pathways

Along the trails where wildflowers bloom,
A fragrant path dispels the gloom.
Each petal whispers tales of old,
In colors vibrant, stories bold.

Through tangled grass and fragrant thyme,
We journey forth, no sense of time.
The air is rich with nature's kiss,
In every breath, we find our bliss.

Beneath the boughs where shadows drape,
We breathe the scent of earth's escape.
Tread lightly on this sacred ground,
Where hidden beauty can be found.

As twilight falls, the scents combine,
Of pine and earth, a soft design.
Through every twist, our spirits soar,
Guided by nature's rich allure.

In this place, our hearts align,
With every breath, the world divine.
The fragrance lingers, pure and free,
On hidden pathways, you and me.

Threads of Life in the Green

In the forest, life entwines,
Each breath a pulse, each leaf a sign.
The threads of green, they intertwine,
In harmony, a grand design.

Roots dig deep in the fertile earth,
Giving rise to life, and birth.
Branches stretch to reach the light,
In the tapestry of day and night.

Every creature plays a part,
Whispers echo, nature's heart.
In the silence, we can hear,
The threads of life, forever near.

Ferns unfurl, and flowers bloom,
Creating joy, dispelling gloom.
In the green, we find our way,
Each thread a moment, here to stay.

Under the canopy, we roam,
Finding peace, we feel at home.
The threads of life, a woven dream,
In the green, forever gleam.

Reverie of the Mossy Floor

In the hush of the twilight glow,
Moss blankets earth, soft and low.
Whispers of secrets, ancient and pure,
Nature's embrace, a tranquil cure.

Beneath trees that sway, roots entwined,
Silent stories of peace we find.
Each step a dream on this verdant bed,
Where echoes of life gently tread.

Sunbeams dance on a dew-kissed leaf,
Time slows down, granting relief.
In this realm where shadows play,
Magic thrives in a soft ballet.

The scent of pine, a soothing balm,
Breath of the forest, serene and calm.
Moments linger, forever stored,
In the heart of the mossy floor.

Here dreams are woven, time stands still,
A haven that soothes, always will.
In nature's lap, souls intertwine,
Lost in reveries, divine design.

Secrets of the Sylvan Sanctuary

Amidst the trees, where shadows fall,
A whispering breeze, a nature's call.
Hidden paths under soft, green boughs,
Secrets entwined in the silent vows.

The brook babbles tales of old,
Of tales and treasures, waiting untold.
Sunlight filters through layers of leaves,
Nature's soul in a tapestry weaves.

Songs of the creatures, wild and free,
Carry the essence of the deep green sea.
Amulets of petals, soft and bright,
Guard the mysteries of the night.

Wandering spirits gather 'round,
In echoes of laughter, joy unbound.
A sanctuary of dreams conceived,
In the heart of the forest, we're believed.

Here lies the magic, the ancient lore,
In the sylvan sanctuary, forevermore.
Embraced by nature's tender hold,
The secrets of the woods unfold.

Dreams in the Forest's Embrace

In the quiet twilight, dreams take flight,
Cradled in shadows, kissed by light.
Whispers of leaves in the summer's breeze,
Nature's lullaby, a peaceful tease.

Mossy carpets cradle every step,
Where the heart wanders, and senses prep.
Timber silhouettes rise, strong and grand,
Guardians of dreams in this enchanted land.

Gentle streams murmur secrets untold,
In rippling echoes, a magic bold.
Stars peek through branches, shyly aglow,
Time drifts softly, a gentle flow.

Within the embrace of trees so wise,
Dreamers awaken to moonlit skies.
Infinite wonders, curious hearts chase,
For each forest is a dreaming place.

Embers of life dance in the night,
In this realm where magic feels right.
Upon nature's canvas, dreams are traced,
Forever cradled in the forest's embrace.

Call of the Resin-Bound Soul

In the depths of the woods, a call so clear,
Resin-bound whispers beckon near.
Tales of the ancients, high and low,
Echoing softly, like river's flow.

With each sticky tear, stories unfold,
Of timeless spirits, both brave and bold.
Captured in amber, secrets bide time,
In the heart of the forest, they silently rhyme.

Roots reach deep where wisdom seeks,
In silence, the language of silence speaks.
The saplings sway, in rhythm divine,
Nature's pulse, a sacred line.

Freed from their shells, the dreams emerge,
To the symphony of life, they surge.
Each branch a portal, each leaf a sigh,
A dance with the stars in the vast, dark sky.

In the sacred woods, we hear the sound,
Of the resin-bound soul, where love is found.
Forever entwined in nature's hold,
A vibrant tale of life retold.

Enchantment of the Pine Needle Rain

In the forest, whispers weave,
Pine needles falling, hearts believe.
Dancing softly on the ground,
Magic in the air is found.

Gentle rain from branches high,
A soothing sound, a sweet lullaby.
Nature draped in shades of green,
Enchantment felt, a tranquil scene.

Each drop sparkles, a fleeting dream,
In the sunlight's softest beam.
Pine needles dance, a tender sway,
Guiding spirits through the day.

Beneath the boughs, we find our peace,
In this realm, our worries cease.
Whispers call, inviting grace,
In the forest's warm embrace.

A world alive with every sound,
In the stillness, love is found.
Enchantment lingers, purest air,
In the pine needle rain, we care.

Symphony of the Swaying Trees

Branches reach towards the sky,
Leaves are dancing, oh so high.
Whispers echo through the wood,
In their motion, life's understood.

Tall and proud, they sway with ease,
Harmonies float upon the breeze.
Nature's song, a sweet refrain,
Each rustle calls, like softest rain.

Roots entrenched in earth so deep,
Guardians of secrets that they keep.
A symphony of life unfolds,
In the magic, stories told.

Sunlight filters, flickers bright,
Casting shadows, dancing light.
Together, trees find their way,
In the symphony of the day.

In each sway, a tale to share,
A connection felt everywhere.
Nature's voice, both strong and free,
Is a melody, a symphony.

Canopy of Silence

Underneath the leafy dome,
Where the wild things feel at home.
A hush settles, a soothing balm,
In this shelter, the world feels calm.

Sunbeams pierce through layers dense,
Creating whispers, pure and immense.
In every corner, tranquility reigns,
Healing hearts, washing pains.

No footfalls break the sacred peace,
In this haven, worries cease.
Nature's breath, a gentle wave,
In silence, the soul we save.

Birds sing softly, echoes blend,
In this stillness, time can bend.
The canopy holds secrets dear,
A sacred space where all draws near.

In the quiet, life's essence flows,
In the silence, true love grows.
Beneath the trees, our spirits align,
In the canopy, hearts intertwine.

Nature's Softest Murmurs

Softly whispers through the leaves,
Nature hums while daylight weaves.
A melody of pure delight,
In the dawn's first gentle light.

Rippling streams and breezy sighs,
Underneath the vast blue skies.
Every moment, tender grace,
Nature's song, a warm embrace.

Rustling grass beneath our feet,
In this realm, we feel complete.
Murmurs cradle, secrets shared,
In the wild, we're truly spared.

Echoes dance on waves of air,
Indigo skies, without a care.
Nature's voice, both kind and wise,
In softest murmurs, joy will rise.

As day turns to night, stars gleam,
In the silence, we can dream.
Nature's heart, forever pure,
In her whispers, we find our cure.

Echoes Among the Evergreens

Whispers rise in the cool night air,
Beneath the stars, a world so rare.
Tall pines sway, their secrets shared,
In every breath, the forest cared.

Footsteps soft on a mossy bed,
Nature's chorus, a tale widespread.
Echoes call from the shadows deep,
In this haven, silence sleeps.

Moonbeams dance through branches high,
Casting dreams where shadows lie.
Each rustle holds a story spun,
In the realm where all begun.

A gentle breeze carries the song,
Of ancient trees where we belong.
Among the evergreens, we roam,
In every splendor, we find home.

So let us wander, hand in hand,
Embrace the magic of this land.
In the echoes, we find our way,
As night surrenders to the day.

Shadows of the Swaying Boughs

Underneath shadows, boughs entwine,
A tapestry where our dreams align.
Rustling leaves sing soft and low,
In nature's arms, we feel the flow.

Sunlight spills through the canopy,
Creating paths for you and me.
Whispers weave in the gentle breeze,
Among the great, ancient trees.

Each fluttering wing, a fleeting grace,
Hides secrets in this sacred space.
The earth beneath, a grounding bed,
In shadows soft, our worries shed.

Time stands still where silence reigns,
In the shade, where peace remains.
The world outside fades away,
In boughs' embrace, we choose to stay.

With every breath, our spirits soar,
In the dance of nature's lore.
Our hearts entwined in nature's vow,
Together, we live in the now.

Secrets Hidden in the Canopy

Above our heads, the branches weave,
Stories told that we believe.
Secrets sheltered in the green,
Mysteries of the unseen.

Birds chirp tales of days gone by,
While leaves whisper a soft sigh.
In the canopy, life does thrive,
In every moment, we feel alive.

Sunlight dapples where shadows play,
Nature unfolding in a ballet.
Ancient roots hold wisdom old,
Embrace the warmth in the cold.

A hidden world above the ground,
With every rustle, magic found.
Climb higher up, explore the heights,
Where secrets linger, out of sights.

Together, we'll discover thoughts,
In tangled brews, life intertwines.
Each heartbeat echoes with the trees,
In their whispers, we find our peace.

Murmurs of the Forest's Heart

Deep in the woods, where shadows dwell,
The forest breathes, weaves its spell.
Murmurs rise from the soil below,
In every heartbeat, nature's glow.

Dancing leaves in the golden light,
Reveal the magic of day and night.
Through every path, the whispers roam,
In this embrace, we feel at home.

Branches reaching for the sky,
Underneath, where secrets lie.
Life unfurls with each passing breeze,
In this haven, our souls find ease.

The pulse of life, a steady beat,
In every moment, feel it sweet.
Together, let's follow the trail,
In the forest's heart, we can't fail.

Let us wander among the trees,
In the hush, we feel the peace.
Murmurs guide us ever near,
In the heart of the woods, we're clear.

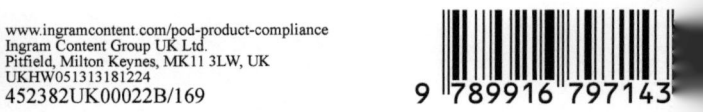

www.ingramcontent.com/pod-product-compliance
Ingram Content Group UK Ltd.
Pitfield, Milton Keynes, MK11 3LW, UK
UKHW051313181224
452382UK00022B/169

9 789916 797143